Meditations *for Adoptive* *Parents*

Meditations for Adoptive Parents

Vernell Klassen Miller

Drawings by
Esther Rose Graber

HERALD PRESS
Scottdale, Pennsylvania
Waterloo, Ontario

Library of Congress Cataloging-in-Publication Data
Miller, Vernell Klassen, 1950-
   Meditations for adoptive parents / Vernell Klassen Miller.
     p. cm.
   Includes bibliographical references.
   ISBN 0-8361-3606-3
    1. Adoptive parents—Prayer-books and devotions—English.
2. Christian life—1960- I. Title.
BV4529.1.M55 1992
242'.645—dc20

92-18480
CIP

1 2 3 4 5 6 7 8 9 10 98 97 96 95 94 93 92

Joyfully dedicated to the first one who
addressed his heavenly Father
precisely as he did his adoptive
father—"Abba" (Daddy). His name is
Jesus. We thank him for providing
adoption for our family and for
walking through it with us—for he has
been this way before.

Author's Preface

There are depths of the human spirit which words cannot plumb, certain experiences which cannot be wrapped in speech. Special hugs, seeing one's children for the first time, or laying a loved one's body to rest in a grave defy verbal expression. They are holy experiences—set apart for God to interpret.

I approach adoption with the same reverence. Each family is unique; I do not presume to address every situation. Yet within adoption's scale, there are certain harmonies which resonate, certain truths which ring clear no matter how vastly our experiences differ. Reverence is the response called forth by such realities as the joy of our children becoming our own; the sorrow of relinquishment or infertility; the ecstasy of Christmas with family; and little, everyday problems and victories. In struggling to wrap words around themes like these, I often sat wordless at my word-processor and wept.

Then I asked Christ, the Word of God become flesh, to breathe life into these meditations and to use them for his purposes. Always I kept in mind his adoption by Joseph the carpenter—because it was through Jesus' adoption into the human family that he made possible our adoption into his heavenly family. Ultimately, that's what makes adoption a holy experience: it is a model of redemption.

To those who reviewed the manuscript, offered suggestions, and wept with me—thank you. To Helen Good Brenneman, author of *Meditations for the Expectant Mother* and *Meditations for the New Mother*—how I have enjoyed giving your books as gifts! It was giving them to adoptive families that caused me to wish for a book like *Meditations for Adoptive Parents*. Thank you. And to those who will read the finished book—when my words run out or seem inadequate, I pray that you will sense the Word beside you, making your own experiences holy, and wrapping them with joy.

—Vernell Klassen Miller
Hanston, Kansas

Contents

III. FAMILY LIFE

The Decision to Adopt

"Enlarge the place of your tent. . . ."
Isaiah 54:2

"Sing, O barren woman,
you who never bore a child;
burst into song, shout for joy,
you who were never in labor;
because more are the children of the
desolate woman
than of her who has a husband,"
says the Lord.
"Enlarge the place of your tent,
stretch your tent curtains wide,
do not hold back;
lengthen your cords,
strengthen your stakes.
"For you will spread out to the right and
to the left;
your descendants will dispossess
nations
and settle in their desolate cities."
Isaiah 54:1-3

Thank You, God, for Friends

*Now faith is being sure of what we hope for and
certain of what we do not see.*
Hebrews 11:1

Brilliant bursts of light shot through the curtains and awakened me to another day of childlessness. I resented the sun, shining so brightly, oblivious to the fact that my days and months were darkened by my husband's and my inability to conceive a child. I had a mother's heart, and the shadow of a mother with empty arms haunted me wherever I went.

"Lord, if it is not your plan for us to have children, then please take this desire away," I would pray, then deliberately turn my thoughts to other activities. Until I saw a child again. So Paul and I "borrowed" children—nephews rode tractor with him, children from our church went fishing with us, young neighbors baked cookies with me, and I taught children at school.

But the desire for a family never went away. And nothing the doctors could do would help; so we prayed for a miracle. We believed God and faith could supply what our physical bodies lacked.

One day when Judy, a teacher friend of mine, left baby Kendee at our home for child care. She said, "I thought you might be interested in some literature I have on adoption."

I hesitated. "But we're praying for a miracle."

"I don't doubt miracles," Judy assured me. "But until one comes, why don't you read this information? Don't wait too long to respond, because it's getting harder and harder to adopt."

How could we have known that that day brought the beginning of our miracle! I shall forever thank the Lord for the sun which heralded the day and for my friend who pointed us in the direction of our children.

Thank You, God, for friends, and thank you for honoring our faith in unexpected ways. Amen.
Prayer Focus: *Thankfulness for friends*

PROMISES

I heard the voice of Jesus say
My child, you must not cry,
For I in my own wisdom
Know the reason why.

Though years have come and gone
Since happiness you've known,
I will restore the wasted years:
You see, you're still my own.

Thank you, God, for promises
Recorded in your Word,
That hope, once lost, can be regained
By trusting in the Lord.[1]

—Shirley Collins

Adoption—Nature's Way

The wolf will live with the lamb, the leopard will lie down with the goat, the calf and the lion and the yearling together; and a little child will lead them.
Isaiah 11:6

Natural enemies becoming friends is a favorite picture of the coming kingdom when all of nature will be restored to peace. Though sin marred the first picture, God preserved a layer of unity which surfaces in adoption whenever mutual needs can be met.

One of our pups mothered a litter of kittens. We have a picture of a cat nursing her adopted rabbits. A rabbit mother took pity on some chicks when their mother died—she sat on them to keep them warm.

In the mysteries of nature lie clues to redemption and to God's own outreach to strangers, outcasts, the fatherless and motherless, and sinners. God calls the little creatures and implants within their instincts the tendency to care for and defend young who were not born to them nor even to their species. Then surely God has placed in the human heart the capability and desire to take a child by choice into the family relationship and make it one's own.

Since God cares for innocent animals and makes provision for their earthly needs through adoption, we know he provides for the needs of people, made in God's image. Jesus also claimed strangers and outcasts as his ancestors and as children of Abraham. He said God cares for the birds of the air and even more for people.

Adoption is not the exception; it is not strange or unusual. It is built into nature and has its root in God's heart. God offers us, with arms wide open, a welcome into his family.

Heavenly Father, I am so grateful that you adopted me into your family. I pray for those who are still seeking for a family, for those who haven't found their home in you yet. Thank you for the examples of adoption in your written Word and in the pages of nature which assure us of your care. Amen.

Prayer Focus: *For peace on earth, in families, in nature, and with God*

A Crucial Point

The idea of being adopted into God's family is a prominent feature in the apostle Paul's description of the Christian life and salvation. Paul uses adoption (Greek: *huiothesia*) five times in this connection, all referring to our relationship to God as Christians. Though the Greek word clearly refers to adoption, English versions translate *huiothesia* in different ways. Most English translations use "adoption" in Romans 8:23 and Galatians 4:5; but Romans 8:15 and 9:4 use the English word "sonship" while Ephesians 1:5 is translated "to be his sons." The interchangeability of "adopted sonship" and "non-adopted sonship" reflects both the Christian and Roman legal understanding that the relationship is identical.[2]

—*Muriel B. Dennis*

In Time of Drought

All Scripture is God-breathed and is useful for teaching. . . .
2 Timothy 3:16

My husband is laying irrigation pipes in hopes of saving our withering corn. Even the hardy buffalo grass has turned brown in the drought.

An area in adoption's landscape has been similarly scorched. One perennial theme is to watch out for the "Ishmaels" and for the inevitable conflicts between children born into a family and those who adopted into it.

Like other illustrations taken from the Bible to discourage adoption, this one has been taken out of context. Ishmael was conceived by Abraham and a surrogate mother, Hagar, who did not have a choice in the matter. She was Sarah's maid and part-time mistress to Abraham. Her continual presence helped complicate matters for everyone—hardly a typical adoption scene where children by birth and by adoption belong equally to both parents!

Actually, I have found the Bible to be my best study book about adoption and my most consistent source of reassurance when facing the dry winds of prejudice. Consider Romans 11. In it Paul teaches that all Christians are also Jews by adoption into a holy root system, that some natural branches fall, that this tree has both natural and grafted branches, that adoption is successful because of faith, that one shouldn't be conceited because of adoption, that being part of the family by adoption or by birth is an act of grace—of election.

This and many other Scriptures tell me that children by adoption are sons and daughters of full stature. God's pattern is that they inherit, receive, and grow as explained in Romans 8, where we as Christians are declared joint heirs with Christ. (He shares the rights and privileges of sonship with us.) God has adopted us, not on a temporary basis, but permanently. He is not taking care of us on behalf of someone else.

Lord, give us openness to your Spirit, which will prevent our own ideas from distorting your Word. Thank you. Amen.

Prayer Focus: *For wisdom to interpret the Bible correctly*

A Beacon

A young woman of an ethnic minority won a beauty contest she didn't choose to enter. Soon after, she married the proud and wealthy ruler of more than 120 provinces from India to Ethiopia—but she did not disclose her background to him. (This woman had been adopted by an uncle who worked for the monarch. He advised her to keep her origins secret, at least for a while.)

Questions and uncertainty must have followed her. Why had her birthparents died? Why had she been adopted? Why had she been brought up in a foreign country? How could God have directed her to this marriage?

Yet by submitting her "rights" to the Lord—thus risking death—she discovered God's plan. Her questions were answered, and her life's purpose was fulfilled.

Legislation was introduced which would have annihilated the people of her ethnic group. At that moment, her adoptive father urged her to reveal her identity. He spoke these immortal words. "If you refrain from speaking on behalf of this group of people, the Lord will send deliverance from somewhere else (but you, yourself, will perish). Who knows but that you were brought into the kingdom for such a time as this!"

So Queen Esther heroically faced the absolute ruler of Persia and Media—her husband, Ahasuerus. She told him her life's story and begged for mercy. The Jewish people still celebrate, in a feast called Purim, the deliverance she won for them.

Mordecai's words stand as a beacon for all who have been adopted. Surely God has called them to a specific family and a specific country for a specific reason. Perhaps "for such a time as this!"

The book, *The Adopted Child Comes of Age,* refutes the idea that parents favor birth children over adopted ones. "Neither the adoptee's ordinal place in the family nor the presence or absence of younger brothers or sisters, whether natural or adopted, showed any apparent association with the adopters' feeling this was their child."[3]

"It's not the bearing so much as the caring that makes one a mother," according to one person. The book *Adoption—Is It for You?* quotes this mother and goes on to say, "Ultimately only one who has [given birth to] a child can fully understand the wonder of biological parenthood. Only one who has adopted a child can fully understand the miracle that makes a particular child yours alone. Only one . . . fortunate enough to experience both can fully understand why biological and adoptive parenthood are so much alike."[4]

Blood Relatives

Myths and endless genealogies . . . promote controversies
rather than God's work—which is by faith.
1 Timothy 1:3-4

I become a mother bear in defense of my cubs and their heritage when I hear unfounded questions and easy answers for complex situations. It seems that building a family by adoption threatens many people—as though they believe that if their family lacked an awareness of genetic relatedness, there would be no other relatedness. They claim that people on every side of adoption are prone to feelings of disconnectedness, rejection, and low self-esteem. Some are. But research shows that these feelings are more common in families built only by birth! (If biological bonds insure stable families, where do all the children in foster care come from?)

A more penetrating question would be, "If rejection is perceived, what causes it? A lack of some genetically inherited bond?"

I doubt it. I believe a sense of security is imparted and not inherited. As children judge by others' reactions whether they are perceived as beautiful or homely, so do they learn whether or not they belong. An adopting couple's belief that bonding is genetically linked would probably hinder a harmonious family relationship. The adoption itself would not cause the problems—but the self-fulfilling beliefs would.

Christians can agree that the Bible advises us not to place too much emphasis on genealogies. Our focus is rather to be on the importance of faith. Without the link of faith, we are not, in an eternal sense, related to our children, whether born to us or adopted. And with faith's linkage, we are blood relatives forever.

Oh, God, help us remember that all relatedness is temporary, unless it is a blood relationship made permanent through Jesus' precious blood. Amen.

Prayer Focus: *For those who feel disconnected from family, friends, and God*

PASSOVER FOR THE FAMILY

Beneath the blood-stained lintel I with my children stand;
A messenger of evil is passing through the land.
There is no other refuge from the destroyer's face:
Beneath the blood-stained lintel shall be our hiding place.

The Lamb of God has suffered, our sins and griefs He bore;
By faith the blood is sprinkled above our dwelling's door.
The foe who seeks to enter doth fear that sacred sign;
Tonight the blood-stained lintel shall shelter me and mine.

My Saviour, for my dear ones I claim Thy promise true
The Lamb is "for the household"—the children's Saviour too.
On earth the little children once felt Thy touch divine;
Beneath the blood-stained lintel Thy blessing give to mine.

O Thou who gave them, guard them—those wayward little feet,
Thy wilderness before them, the ills of life to meet.
My mother love is helpless, I trust them to Thy care!
Beneath the blood-stained lintel, oh, keep me ever there!

The faith I rest upon Thee Thou wilt not disappoint;
With wisdom, Lord, to train them, my shrinking heart anoint.
Without my children, Father, I cannot see Thy face;
I plead the blood-stained lintel, Thy covenant of grace.

Oh, wonderful Redeemer, who suffered for our sake,
When o'er the guilty nations the judgment storm shall break,
With joy from that safe shelter may then meet Thine eye,
Beneath the blood-stained lintel, my children, Lord, and I.[5]

—Jewish Voice

Infertility—Through Loss to Blessing

And we know that in all things God works for the good of those who love him,
who have been called according to his purpose.
Romans 8:28

Jonathan was only three when he put his little arms around my neck and said, "Mommy, I wish I had grown in your body."

His sweet, honest longing brought new revelation to me and tears to my eyes. I held him tightly and whispered something that, in my appreciation of adoption, I thought I would never need to say. "I do too, Sonny."

By then, I no longer felt the need for a biological child. It was a different kind of infertility I sensed at that moment—created by love for this particular boy. I was willing to suffer—even die—for my son. Yet I missed the privilege and pain of giving birth to him.

Our daughter is now three. In our conversations, we discuss pregnancy, birth, and adoption. In a way similar to my discovery of a new infertility, I also found new relatedness to my children. It brought a sense of blessing.

"Why was I born in Oklahoma, Mommy?" It was one of Elise's standard lead-in questions to the story of how she became our daughter. Her round face leaned close to mine, her eyes sparkling in anticipation.

"Another woman got to carry you before you were born," I began.

Then I recognized a special bond my children and I have which not every family has or would see. Our mutual needs propelled us together. Even if conception occurred in our family, even if our children met people genetically related to them, the reality of our unity would never change. The miracle is that our losses have brought us some of life's greatest blessings. That will never change.

Dear God, thank you for miracles. I couldn't have guessed that someday I would thank you for Paul's and my infertility, but that's what drew us toward Jonathan and Elise. Bless the special bonds which draw us together in love. Amen.

Prayer Focus: *Gratitude for family unity*

ON THE NIGHT OF ANDREW'S BIRTH

Strange vigil, this—

My joy subdued
In reverence to her pain
As he,
Traversing unremembered roads of light,
Slips softly
From infinity
Into mortality,
Through her body
To my arms.

Tonight is not for sleep;
It is a night
For fervent thoughts
Projected up and outward
For her,
For him
For me—

As unto her
Our son is born.[6]

—*Margaret Munk*

I've read that every "good" infertility story ends either in a successful pregnancy or at adoption. Perhaps that's not always the case. It may be that God intends to glorify Himself through the life of a childless woman who quietly walks with Him [and] trusts that His love is sufficient. . . .[7]

—*Karolyn Kelly-Keefe*

A Family Affair

Give thanks in all circumstances, for this is God's
will for you in Christ Jesus.
1 Thessalonians 5:18

I hadn't seen Edna—we called her Eddie—since we were 4-Hers on a trip to Washington, D.C., about fifteen years before. Her knock at the door brought laughter and assurances that neither of us "had changed a bit." Hours passed like minutes. After supper, my husband left us like teenage girls, remembering friends and catching up on each other's lives.

My son, Jonathan, had nursed until he slept a peaceful sleep on my lap. Now we focused on him. I enthusiastically related the blessings of adoption and adoptive breastfeeding.

In contrast to her previous bubbly enthusiasm, Eddie sat quietly on the divan. Tears ran unchecked down her face. "I can't tell you what this means to me," she began. "You saw the pictures of my daughters. My oldest . . . well, she's pregnant. She's decided on adoption, and I think it's the right thing . . . I'm so proud of the way she's thinking this through, but—I'm sorry for crying—it's so hard. . . . It's my first grandchild!"

She fought for control. "I've been worried. What we really want for this baby is a family and to be loved. I've asked, 'Will he be loved?' I think I see the answer tonight. Our visit was meant to be."

Relinquishment and adoption touch entire families—not just individuals. Eddie's visit meant a lot to me, too. It placed our family's experiences alongside a birth family's experiences. It gave me the chance to tell someone who needed to hear it of the gratitude I felt toward such a sacrifice. We both cried tears of gratitude.

Lord, thank you for sending others into our lives to bless us. Surround Eddie, her family, and all relinquishing birth families with a sense of your care. Amen.
Prayer Focus: *For extended families on both sides of adoption's picture*

LEGACY OF AN ADOPTED CHILD

Once there were two women
Who never knew each other.
One you do not remember.
The other, you call mother.

Two different lives shaped your one.
One became your guiding star.
The other became your sun.

The first gave you life,
And the second taught you to live in it.
The first gave you the need for love,
And the second was there to give it.

One gave you a nationality.
The other gave you a name.
One gave you the seed of talent.
The other gave you an aim.

One gave you emotions.
The other calmed your fears.
One saw your first sweet smile.
The other dried your tears.

One gave you up—it was all that she could do.
The other prayed for a child,
And God led her straight to you.

And now you ask me through your tears,
The age-old question through the years:

Heredity or environment—which are you the product of?
Neither, my Darling, neither:
Just two different kinds of love![6]

—Author unknown

We are not happy for the circumstances which led to the birth mothers' relinquishment of our children. Christians do not advocate suffering. We are happy, however, that the Lord can redeem any situation, and adoption is one example of that redemption.

Prepare Your Calendar

*And if I go and prepare a place for you, I will come back and take you to be
with me that you also may be where I am.*
John 14:3

Cindy inquired about the wait for our first child. "You need to prepare," she said.

"But it might be two years," I countered.

"Then get a calendar," she insisted. "It probably won't be that long, but mark off each day. Be ready when that child comes!"

I had prepared myself for the long run and for the possibility that there might never be children for us. I did not prepare a room. I stored gifts and hand-me-down items in the garage until the day the phone rang, and my mother's cheerful voice said, "May Dad and I come over to help refinish the baby bed and high chair?"

Expectant adoptive parents have work to do. They differ most from other families in the preparation for parenthood—not in parenthood itself. If infertility has been part of the reason for choosing adoption, facing grief is important. Then, like all expectant parents, the couple needs to dream about the child and engage in "nesting" behavior.

A network of God's people helped me during the crucial waiting for our first child. It was easier for me to believe for our second child. I unpacked some of Jonathan's clothes from storage in case of another boy and bought several pink dresses in case of a girl.

I was not aware my behavior was called "psychological pregnancy." I had not studied its importance and effect on the transition into parenthood. I was aware, however, that our friends and family helped us become parents by doing things for us when we could not do more ourselves.

Dear Lord Jesus, you went to prepare a place for me so I could come live with you some day. Help me understand the tasks before me so I can prepare well for my child, too. I long for his or her arrival. Thank you. Amen.

Prayer Focus: *For the preparation expectant couples must do*

Calendar

Carol A. Hallenback, who developed the study book, *Our Child,* delineates the stages in pregnancy and in adoption.

Biological preparation for parenthood:
1. Pregnancy validation
2. Fetal embodiment into mother's body image
3. Child perceived as separate entity and plans made
4. Role transition into parenthood through birth

Adoptive preparation for parenthood:
1. Adoption accepted as form of childbearing
2. Child embodiment into parents' emotional images
3. Child perceived as a reality and plans made
4. Role transition into parenthood through adoption[9]

Deciding to relinquish a child for adoption is an unforgettable experience. The birthmother typically goes through these three phases:

1. Includes time from pregnancy validation until birth
2. Begins with birth of baby and reevaluation
3. Occurs after the child is placed for adoption[10]

Phase one may include facing a crisis, exploring options, and learning about finances, child care, and adoption. In phase two birthmothers reach a preliminary decision before delivery but need to reevaluate after the baby is born. Understanding and support is critical to the mother's emotional health. Phase three begins after placement. Reentering the world includes establishing new relationships as well as deciding whom to tell and how to respond if someone says, "How could a mother ever do that?" Some birthmothers file a document stating their desire to meet their child at a later date.

Each relinquishment, though sharing similarities with others, is as unique as a fingerprint. Similarly, the steps in adoptive preparation vary widely, depending on such factors as age, international placement, and presence of handicaps. Appreciation of each other is enhanced as we learn about stages of pregnancy, relinquishment, and adoption.

Entitlement

*"Fear not, for I have redeemed you; I have summoned you
by name; you are mine."*
Isaiah 43:1

"Surprise!" Karen shouted as she and other children popped from hiding. Blue ribbons, posters, and a huge banner welcomed us home with our new son. Soon family members made trips from other towns in Kansas, South Dakota, and Texas. We were not alone in the establishment of our family. How interesting it is for me to read—now many years later—what a dramatic effect support systems have in the bonding process!

To reach a sense of *entitlement* (which usually comes with pregnancy and birth) is the next crucial task of adoptive parents. Without it, bonding between parents and child cannot occur.

The ideas most people have today about bonding come from one particular study.[11] Mothers who were given immediate contact with their children after birth and for sixteen extra hours were "more affectionate, more interested in and less harsh with their children." However, as these mothers were studied in later years, there was *no measurable difference* between those who had immediate contact with their children and those for whom contact was delayed. Furthermore, the results of the study have not been substantiated by other studies. Yet the myth that those few hours and days are irreplaceable in the bonding process continues and causes needless anxiety.

There are more vital elements which affect the bonding process. Dorothy W. Smith and Laurie Nehls Sherwem give evidence showing that acceptance by spouse, family, and friends affects bond formation between mother and child more than any other environmental influence—in both biological and adoptive situations.[12]

I'm thankful, Lord, that bonding can occur early or late. Thank you that our children received a hearty welcome, and help me to be supportive of others, too. Amen.
Prayer Focus: *Support for new families*

BY WHAT AUTHORITY?
Broken vessels—none of us "Okay"—
How can we lead our tender ones, day by day?
By what authority do we set limits and teach?
Ah, this is redemption's story—
That in myself is no worth and no glory.
Even mediocrity is beyond my reach!

But I was created according to a plan;
So that what I cannot do, he can!
My areas of weakness through him are made strong.
"Yes, dears," I tell my daughter and son,
"I was wrong, made a mistake, wrecked that one,
But there's more to the story—more to my song—

"God placed you with me—me with you.
He gave Daddy and me an amazing job to do—
*To represent **his** parenthood is our task.*
We stand in his image and feel awed.
For as you obey us, you obey God."
Oh, may his glory shine through my flask!

And may our children grow up to know
That life isn't an accident—God planned it so.
(The question deserves more than mere sentiment.)
As much as I love them, I'll have to agree:
*God's image in **them** is marred, as it is in me.*
Will they blame me for the marring—heredity?
     environment?

Oh, no! Not if I have taught them well.
They'll know better and be able to tell
Their own redemption story—
How they learned to see God's face
And experience his grace
And now, too, reflect his glory.[13]
—Vernell Klassen Miller

Entitlement, Continued

*As a father has compassion on his children, so the Lord
has compassion on those who fear him.*
Psalm 103:13

"Babies don't have much personality," Paul insisted before we had children.

Amazingly, Jonathan became his son the first time he held him. "He's beautiful!" Paul kept saying. "He's the most beautiful baby in the world!"

I reminded Paul of his previous reaction to infants.

"It's different when it's your own," he replied.

In yesterday's meditation, we examined the importance of support for new families. For adoptive parents, another variable in bonding is acquaintance with the birthmother. Some adoptive parents experience bonding to their unborn child through her and count it a privilege to help with the birth. But some who meet the birthmother have trouble moving into true parenthood. This phenomenon is common enough to warrant further research.[14]

Other factors also affect the entitlement process. The sheer amount of work required for many adoptions is a form of "labor." For some, the feeling of belonging develops slowly, along with caregiving and pleasant experiences. Sometimes a crisis or a severe illness endured by parent and child together cements their relationship. For some parents, it's simply "love at first sight."

On our drive home with new baby Elise, Paul reached for my hand and said, "It happened again . . . I mean, about Elise. She's beautiful! I'm so glad we have a son and a daughter!" I still like to tease him about his attitude toward babies. And he still maintains that "they're all the same—unless they're your own!"

Ah, Lord! You have made me your very own! Do you smile when you look at me and think that I am beautiful? Is it possible for me to make you happy like our children delight us? I wonder what it will be like—seeing your face for the first time. . . .

Prayer Focus: *Meditation on God as a compassionate Father, extravagantly in love with his children*

Entitlement, Continued

A child can only bond to someone able to bond back—a parent who claims and is free to identify with him or her.

Here are factors which may influence the bonding process:

Attitudes toward adoption
Level of infertility resolution (if applicable)
Ability to fantasize and plan for the coming child
Type of adoption: Are biological parents known? Is child part of adoptive parents' extended family?
Agency and social worker attitudes toward parents
Amount of control parents feel they have in the process
Presence or absence of supportive people
Age of child at placement
If older—availability of pictures, exchange of information, a previous meeting
Number of children—single or sibling group
Perceived similarities in habits, tastes, or physical appearance
Presence of handicaps, state of health of the child and the adoptive parents
Amount of time spent together
Crisis or severe illness faced together
Personality and temperament of family members
Plus the infinite variety of factors which would affect any family

Not flesh of my flesh
Nor bone of my bone,
But still miraculously my own.
Never forget for a single minute
You didn't grow under my heart—
BUT IN IT![15]

—*Fleur Conkling Heyliger*

Miscarriage—It Happens in Adoption, Too

"The Lord is my shepherd, I shall not be in want."
Psalm 23:1

I wept while reading a story in a newsletter.[16] Adoptive parents were called on to return their baby to the birthmother. The author concluded the story with her hope to conceive their next child—not because birth is better, but because "I don't know if I have the courage for another adoption," she said.

Few adoptions are anxiety-free. The waiting period evokes questions and worries similar to those of pregnancy, plus some unique concerns. What if the agency or lawyer believes something disqualifies us? What if the birthmother changes her mind? What if international policies change before we get our child from another country? A thousand "ifs" lurk in the shadows, threatening "miscarriage" at every stage.

My mother telephoned while I was struggling with application forms and my doubts that we would ever really have children. "How are you?" she asked.

"Well . . . 'dry,' would probably describe it. I'm so numb I can't even pray. I told the Lord if I needed prayer, he'd have to call on someone else to pray for me, 'cause I can't even pray for myself!" I tried to laugh to make it sound less serious.

Mom was quiet. Then she said, "Vernell, that's why I called. Something told me to pray for you. I had to know how you were."

When I hung up the phone, I was not so far under the bottom of the bottom. My Shepherd knew my needs. Being reminded of that filled me with assurance—even if our children never came.

Jesus, my good Shepherd, I will lie down beside still waters tonight, content that you know my needs. Amen.

Prayer Focus: *For those experiencing miscarriage*

The Grief of Adoptive Miscarriage

Miscarriage typically leaves months, even years, of grief in its wake. Ken and Susan Viguers describe another experience with miscarriage. The birthmother decided not to relinquish the child they had prepared for but had not seen. "Our loss was nonetheless a death: a life was taken from us as finally as death takes a life. . . . After all, we did have a child, if only briefly, and the means by which we bore that child made no difference in our feelings. . . . [W]e found that the assumption we [had] shared with so many people—that adoption was second best—had vanished. We knew better—if only by the measure of our grief."[17]

TEARS IN SEASON

I was down—
all the way
below the bottom
of the bottom.

I don't know how
I got up.
I remember weeping
a long time—
until someone
wept with me.

Then
my weeping stopped[18]

—Marilyn Black Phemister

Solomon and the Real Mother

A reading based on 1 Kings 3:16-28

To be loved was all I really wanted, but my circumstances were hard. I made bad choices. A single woman in my society didn't have many career options, especially if her family wasn't wealthy. By prostitution, I could support myself and my elderly parents. But I couldn't develop lasting friendships. I felt alienated, depressed, cut off from the mainstream of life.

When my baby came, he meant everything to me. He made me feel important. I needed and loved him more than I thought I could love anyone. I wished for him a better life than I could offer; I often dreamed of what he might become.

Like other mothers, I slept with my baby so that I could nurse him during the night as he desired. Such a peaceful babe! I wanted this stage to last forever.

One morning before dawn, terror struck. The babe was cold. Had I rolled over and suffocated him? I clutched his lifeless body to my chest and screamed. My own life might as well have ended. My purpose for living was dead, my most important person gone.

But something felt strange. I sensed this wasn't my son. Someone else had him—and I had someone else's child!

My hysteria wakened the neighbors. They lit lamps and came running to calm me. I was not to be calmed! Of course they didn't believe I had been tricked. Why should they? Any other mother in my circumstances would be unreasonable. The other woman in the house had a newborn also.

We were dragged in to see King Solomon. My screaming was silenced when his servants carried in a saber and cutting block. I thought I might be the victim, so the rest of the world could have peace again. I welcomed death if I couldn't have my son.

That was when I first looked at the king. Though he was scrutinizing us two distraught women, his face was calm. How could he be so peaceful when he was mistaken? He had misjudged me. My co-workers had wronged me. As hope died in me, I fell on the cold stone and closed my eyes, awaiting relief from misery.

I heard the footsteps of two men coming in my direction. Each second seemed like an eternity. I waited. And waited. But they never touched me. Instead, I heard my son scream. That cry could have brought me back from hell. They had laid him on the chopping block. No force on earth could have stopped me then. I flew to his side.

What unearthly reasoning had led to this? The guards grabbed and held me back.

New screams from the bottom of my soul pierced the courtroom, matched the intensity of my son's screams, and rose above them. I accused, railed, blasphemed, and cursed everyone and every wrong ever done to me. I begged them to kill me but let my son live.

King Solomon gazed at me. Sure I was out of my mind. I had just proved it!

The other woman stood calmly.

The king spoke quietly. "As I said, divide the baby. Give half to each mother."

How I hated the other woman standing there, as defiled as I in every way, a thief and a liar, too. And now a murderer. She would rather let a newborn die than admit she was wrong. I spat at her. She did not deserve the title of "woman," much less "mother."

Then I gathered all my courage—more than I knew I had. For the first time in hours, I spoke in a clear tone. My mind was made up. I would deny everything I knew and wanted and believed in to save my son.

"No, King, you are wrong." I stood straighter. "You must not kill an innocent child for the sake of us two ignoble women." I felt sudden relief at admitting my own sinfulness. "You don't believe he is my son. But I have been mistrusted before. I can live with that. I could never live thinking I could have spared his life." My eyes left the king's kind face. I forced out a whisper. "Give him. . . . Give him to . . . her."

Then sobs blinded my eyes, wracked my body, and reduced me to a crumpled heap again. "I love you, son! Please know I did this because I want you to live!"

I had never loved like that before. I was transformed as I realized that no human could make a greater sacrifice. I had denied myself for the sake of another. New worth crept into every cell of my body. My sobbing subsided. I lay there, weak and helpless, but somehow pure and noble, on the floor at the feet of the king.

I had died. But I was born again. I could never go back to my former work. My heart felt both torn out by grief yet filled with new resolve. I almost wanted to thank the king.

Everything became so quiet. I turned and glanced up at King Solomon. He had tears in his eyes and my son in his arms.

He looked at me steadily, then said, "Give the babe to her. She is the real mother."

Truth sailed across the room as he spoke. He had not determined who had given birth to the boy—had not even asked! He had only determined who loved him.

I held my child gratefully and tightly to myself and looked with new understanding at the king. I sensed justice and righteousness and goodness. I at last knew love.

This woman's example and the king's standard of love challenge all lesser definitions of a "real" mother. Realness is not based on biology or law. It is comprised of love.

—*Vernell Klassen Miller*

Homecoming

"You have received a spirit of adoption."
Romans 8:15

For you did not receive a spirit of slavery to fall back into fear, but you have received a spirit of adoption. When we cry, "Abba! Father!" it is that very Spirit bearing witness with our spirit that we are children of God, and if children, then heirs, heirs of God and joint heirs with Christ—if, in fact, we suffer with him so that we may also be glorified with him.

Romans 8:15-17, NRSV

Homecoming

This is the day the Lord has made; let us rejoice and be glad in it.
Psalm 118:24

I fell in love with baby Jonathan—not just a little, but 100 percent. Even his sweet baby smell intoxicated me. With my husband's wonderful encouragement and the use of a nursing aid, I was able to breastfeed him (and later our daughter). During those early months of holding and rocking him, happy tears washed away years of sorrow.

The preparation period is suddenly over, whether or not its tasks were completed. Ideally, the new parents feel secure in their role. They are ready to invest emotionally in their child, provide daily care, and offer authority and discipline. Friends, neighbors, and family are enthusiastic.

In reality, each parent-child bond is different. Establishing a family relationship with older children is a conscious, two-way process. It may involve grieving the loss of foster parents and siblings, an orphanage, the country of birth, even one's language or name. For any new family, the homecoming may be a mixture of joy and fatigue, anticipation and worry, pleasure and pain. For most adoptive families, it is also a day of inexpressible gratitude that obstacles have been overcome and the long-awaited privilege of parenting is at hand.

With the arrival of our baby, the house became a happy mess. True to their style, my parents called. "Leave some work for us," they said. A teenage neighbor, Kristi, folded the laundry and sometimes kissed the baby shirts before putting them away. When our washing machine quit, Grandpa Miller invited us to use his. Once when Jonathan and I drove in to Grandpa's farm, his long-sleeved cotton work shirts hung from his clothesline—and beside them dozens of freshly washed diapers flapped in the breeze.

Although becoming a mother rocked my sanity, I will always cherish those memories. And I will always be grateful to the angels of mercy who took the mountains of work and wrapped us with golden deeds as we became a family.

Dear God, is there a new family with a stack of laundry which I could transform into a golden deed today?
Prayer Focus: *Gratitude for angels*

Adoptive Families Are Better Adjusted

As an adoptive parent, you've undoubtedly heard from many sources—including usually reliable magazines—that people who have been adopted are somehow "different." For many years, it seemed that every adoption researcher asserted that not only were they different but the adoptive parents were to blame.

It now looks like such views may be wrong. Kathlyn Marquis and Richard Detweiler, researchers at Drew University, have taken a careful look at a group of adopted and nonadopted persons. An article based on their findings states, "On seven separate measures . . . adopted persons rated their parents as superior, compared to their nonadopted peers." People who have been adopted see themselves as more in control of their lives than nonadopted people. They also have more favorable views of other people than those who have not been adopted.

The article reports that in trying to explain the discrepancy between these new and earlier findings, the researchers pondered these factors.

First, their subjects were drawn from a normal community population, not a clinic population. Second, psychiatric consensus has been shown to be inaccurate in a number of areas of behavior (studies of nearly 30 years ago showed that psychologists were no more accurate than secretaries in diagnostic accuracy and a 1968 study showed there were almost six times greater diagnostic error by psychiatrists than by students). Third, they think that it is possible that social changes have created a more positive view of adoption: "gradually adoption has become more acceptable and less often something to be hidden." Thus, adoptive parents might now provide a healthier psychological environment.

The researchers themselves summarized results of their study in these memorable words: "There is not a shred of evidence . . . that indicates any of the previously reported negative characteristics of dependency, fearfulness, tenseness, hostility, loneliness, insecurity, abnormality, inferiority, poor self-image, or lack of confidence."[19]

This Is the Day Which the Lord Has Made

*I praise you because I am fearfully and wonderfully made;
your works are wonderful, I know that full well.*
Psalm 139:14

Zola Levitt summarized the seven feasts of Israel and compared them to corresponding developmental stages of the unborn child. For example, the feast of trumpets, celebrated in the seventh month, called field workers and others who could hear it to the temple for a holy convocation. By the first day of the seventh month, an unborn child's hearing is developed, and he or she correctly discriminates sound.[20] Zola's parallels fascinated me; I enjoyed imagining God celebrating as he created my child. This is a tribute I wrote for Elise.

And so you come to me, my daughter, having been so recently fashioned in harmony with the feasts of Israel. I rejoice in the freshness of your creation, and looking into your guileless face, I see reflections of God.

So far, you have celebrated without me. Now we will celebrate together. Your daddy and I will tell you the stories behind Jewish and Christian rituals. We will add our own yet-to-be-discovered traditions.

We will tell and retell the story of your beginnings, of our first meeting, our trip home, your dedication in church, our adoption day in court. We will look forward to culminating our celebrations someday at a banquet with the Lord in his heavenly kingdom. Until then, we will celebrate life. Starting today—this! The first of our life together!

Prayer: "*My soul magnifies the Lord, and my heart rejoices within me!*" *This is a holy day for me. Today I saw my daughter for the first time. Gazing into the face of my child, I lose desire for everything else, and the time passes imperceptibly. I can imagine only one thing which can surpass this moment: seeing your face for the first time, Lord. I worship you. In awe and wonder and profound gratitude, I worship you. Amen.*

Prayer Focus: *Praise and celebration*

HEY, MOM! WE'RE HOME!

A shuffle of feet, the slam of a door,
I've heard this sound many times before.
Yet of this noise I never weary,
For with it comes a cheery
"Hey, Mom! We're home!"

When home sometimes becomes a riot,
I may long for peace and quiet.
Yet when all day they've been away,
I'm very happy to hear them say,
"Hey, Mom! We're home!"

When I reach my home up yonder,
May I never have to wonder
If my children too have found the way.
Please, dear God, once more let me hear them say,
"Hey, Mom! We're home!"[21]

—Mrs. Roman Liechty

Ken and Valorie have children both by birth and adoption. Valorie says, "There's not much difference in becoming parents to a newborn, whether the child comes by birth or adoption. But for us, the bonding process is different with an older child. I'd say after about two and a half years, the child has conscious memories and past relationships to deal with. Adjustment becomes a deliberate effort for both parents and child. But regardless of how they come to us, we parents need to remember our children are only on loan to us from God. . . ."[22]

We Are Born Together

He called a little child and had him stand among them. And he said: "I tell you the truth, unless you change and become like little children, you will never enter the kingdom of heaven."
Matthew 18:2-3

I have noticed other parents responding in awe to the tender bundle of a newborn, so small it seems to disappear in their arms, as if inside a nest. Could this small body really house an entire, complete, immortal human being?

My soul wraps itself around my daughter with gossamer promises to protect and nourish; with outrageous, impossible promises to be everything to her she'll ever need, to keep her from all evil; with layer upon layer of promises enfolding my little angel, my owlet in my nest; with promises and prayers, thanksgivings and pleadings, songs and silence.

I am changed. In fear and trembling I sense the challenge of parenting, of guiding this person toward the noble, highest things in life. The challenge compels me to move to greater things myself, to be more than I have been before, to risk impossible dreams, to believe in the Almighty God more firmly than ever.

My daughter awakes. Her eyes hold mine in a strong, steady, unrelenting gaze. The moment is holy. As her brother did three years before, she assesses me, absorbing something from my soul, asking questions only my heart can answer. The air around us seems to fill with the intensity of the moment, and I can bear no more. I glance away, then gaze again into the soul of my daughter. We are born together, and I am exhausted.

Heavenly Father, I lie here in your holy presence, exhausted again by the child-bearing of adoption. Becoming a parent has reduced me to a child myself . . . aware of my weakness, inabilities, incompleteness. Help me to rely on you completely, like my children depend on me. Give me new strength, new wisdom, and new faith. Amen.

Prayer Focus: *Strength for new families and that they will have time to rest*

WE ARE BORN TOGETHER

I sit down to snuggle you in my arms,
In my warm nest, my little owlet.
The leaves of the forest shelter us,
Shelter our nestling, our birthing,
Shelter our becoming, our adoption,
Our growth to a new identity—
A change for us both:
For you, a new heritage, a new soil for faith,
For me, a new person, a new mother.
We will nestle, and when we emerge,
Our identities will have blended.

—Vernell Klassen Miller

And One Note of Caution:

Oneness—too much—can be dangerous,
because we may want the child to become
little images of ourselves.[23]

—Eleanor Niemela Beachy

The Blessing

Bless me—me too, my father!
Genesis 27:34b

"Who was the woman who took good care of me until you came?" Elise asked at dinner one day. "Let's count how many mothers I have."

"Okay. First of all, your birthmother kept you warm and safe before you were born."

One chubby finger went up.

"Then your foster mother held you and fed you until we could come for you."

Another finger up.

"Then your Mommie came. I'm your adoptive mother."

Finger number three.

"You also have two grandmothers—Grandma Miller is waiting for you in heaven, and Grandma Klassen is baking some pies for you in Goessel."

Fingers four and five.

I tend to think of myself as my children's only mother, and in their experience, I am. Yet I believe it is important for me to impart to them a sense of the blessings which began before I held them in my arms. That is the foundation from which they build their understanding of adoption. When they learn more about factors behind relinquishment, I want them already to know they have always been greatly loved. I want them already to have a sense of destiny in God's plan for the world.

As adoptive parents honor their children's first parents when talking about them, they enable the children to feel good about themselves. In cases where children are older when adopted and the new family may resent actions of biological parents, the adoptive parents need to explain that whatever happened was not because the child was bad. God's care and protection can be talked about, and thanks can be given that the children are now in a home where they can experience his healing and love.

Jesus, the one who redeems the past and restores souls, give our children an awareness of your goodness, which has continually surrounded them. Amen.

Prayer Focus: *That we might incorporate elements of godly blessing every day*

Good News

What do children say in response to various questions about adoption, including what it's like to have adoptive parents who look different than the child?[24]

"If she were green, it wouldn't matter. She's still my mother."

"Everything has gone fine for me, so there is nothing more to say. I am not bothered about my background—Mum and Dad are my parents, and that's that."

"I like it because I have my own family."

"You have something to be very proud of."

"It's a bother when people ask why my parents are white and I'm not."

"Adopting a brother? It's the 'fun-est' thing!"

"Being adopted is a very wonderful thing that the Lord made it happen to me. It was a very scary experience because I didn't know how long it would last. Knowing I have people that really care for me and that I really care for is a very great blessing."

"Adoption means you make something yours."

"Adoption means you belong."

"I know what it's like without a mother."

Good news: an important finding of Dorothy Smith and Laurie Sherwen's research was the overwhelmingly positive view of adoption—especially noteworthy because their sample included "many older children, handicapped children, and children whose race or ethnicity differed from that of their adoptive parents. Some of these adoptive situations were clearly high risk from the standpoint of bonding theory. Nevertheless, most mothers and children seemed to be coping well."[25] Families are resilient. Initial complexities were not an accurate indicator of later adjustment and family solidarity.

Secure Relationships

God sets the lonely in families. . . .
Psalm 68:6

"I give Vernell back to you, Lord," Mother prayed at my high school graduation. As each of their children reached that milestone, she and Dad considered their role as primary authorities in our lives completed. They had laid the foundation of Jesus Christ, and we would build on it.

Each home develops its own style of differentiation—that is, the process of children becoming independent and assuming autonomous, adult responsibilities. To feel secure in relationships and to develop a self-concept are two main tasks of childhood. Then the separation process continues at each stage of development, with the child continually taking more responsibility.

Blocks to bonding cause later problems in "letting go." Children who do not experience the bond of a stable parent-child relationship are anxious about losing other relationships as well. Fear of loss may be too great to risk, so efforts at establishing close friendships are minimal. In this case what may look like differentiation cannot be, since there is no relationship from which to separate. The veneer of independence hides vulnerability to pain.

If, however, the earlier stages of bonding and growth have been satisfactory, the young adult faces the task of establishing a separate identity (in addition to the identity previously enjoyed as part of the family).

Surprise! The person who has experienced a nurturing adoptive relationship may be ahead of non-adopted peers in this task. Some differences between family members may be obvious. Others have been talked about. A clear sense of selfhood can develop when families express appreciation of individuality, in contrast to families with predetermined, rigid expectations of each other.

Dear Lord, designer of the paths I walk in, adoption enhances my understanding of life. Help me to use my experience to help others. Amen.
Prayer Focus: *Thanks for the advantages of adoption*

KINSHIP

Why?
The white-haired matriarch demanded.
Why graft this brown-skinned child
Into your family tree,
A tropic pineapple
Upon a bough of temperate pears?
Choose one at least
Who looks like you.
This one is not your son.

In pride of family,
She has forgotten
To be prouder still;
Forgotten that their family,
And mine,
Is large
And ancient,
And of royal lineage.

She is right
That he is not my son.
he is my brother.[26]

—Margaret Munk

Accountability

Let us throw off everything that hinders.
Hebrews 12:1

"Can you home school your children?" a friend once asked me. "I thought that since they had been adopted, you might not be allowed to."

I was shocked. I have every legal right of parenthood.

Yesterday's meditation touched on differentiation for young people. Adoptive parents have a separating to accomplish also—from our real and perceived benefactors in the adoption process. During the period of gathering credentials for parenthood, we adoptive couples sooner or later realize we are at the mercy of others' judgment of our ability to parent.

Many times a fond, respectful relationship develops between the adoptive couple and the agency or individuals handling the adoption. But such relationships can place the potential adoptive parents in a dependent position. Adoptive couples tend to feel grateful to those who have helped facilitate the adoption, particularly to the birthmother.

One task, then, in moving from the "childbearing" stage of adoption to actual parenting is to assume full responsibility for the child who is now legally and emotionally ours. Contact and friendship with the lawyer or agency can still be maintained. But it must now be on the level of equals. The decision to place the child has been made. Authority has been transferred. For better or worse, the child is now ours.

Incomplete transfer of parental rights can hinder bonding, discipline, and family identity. Yet even when the transfer is understood by those involved in the adoption, families may be surprised by the number of people who assume certain rights and privileges are granted only through physical conception and birth.

Here again, we find that adoptive parents may have an advantage in helping children grow steadily more independent. It's a task we accomplished more than once!

Lord, I lay aside the weights and restrictions of those who do not understand adoption, but I always want to be accountable to you. Amen.

Prayer Focus: *To accept children as loans from God and to be accountable to him*

Perspectives—

- When I discuss common problems about my children, I am not ungrateful nor questioning adoption. Adoption isn't so fragile that we have to be perfect. Our families won't fall apart if we admit frustration with each other.

- I hope other people are comfortable when I share about our experiences. Others talk about their pregnancies and births as normal aspects of family life. Adoption is part of *our* family, and hiding it would be abnormal.

- We explain what being genetically related means. But "being related" for our children usually means being in a relationship—by love, law, family composition; or by sharing beliefs, hobbies, interest.

"You can tell I'm part Klassen," Jonathan once exclaimed as he demonstrated an ability peculiar to our family.

Grandpa Klassen laughed. "No, my family didn't get that from me! That shows you're part Strausz!" (Grandma's side)

- Many habits and characteristics are learned behaviors. Like other parents, we enjoy noting similarities within our family. We also enjoy our children's differences and special features which we couldn't have passed on to them. Then there are inherited features which happen to match ours.

Grandpa Miller, Elise, and I were eating at a restaurant when Elise's baby antics caught the attention of a fellow diner. "She's so cute," he told me. "I can tell she got her nose from you!"

"That was nice of him to say," I whispered to Grandpa. "But I don't know how she would have gotten her nose from me!" We chuckled about that throughout the meal.

Affirmative Adoption Language

*"May the words of my mouth and the meditation of my heart be pleasing
in your sight, O Lord, my Rock and my Redeemer."*
Psalm 19:14

A writer friend, Marilyn, and I anticipated a week at the Christian Bookseller's Association convention in Denver, where waiting in long lines produces weary feet. Muscular dystrophy confines her to a wheelchair.

"At least you'll be sitting!" I joked.

"You'd be surprised how many people say that to me. And you don't know how gross it sounds to someone who would love to get aching feet by standing up! Bottoms get tired, too, you know, and I'm stuck in one position," she snapped.

No, I didn't know how that sounded. I was glad she told me. My impulsive verbal interactions with other people sometimes miss the mark. I will seek to obey the Bible's admonition to be careful of the words I speak.

Susan T. Viguer, notes the verbal abuse adoptive families contend with. "Nicholas and Ruth are children of our own. . . . There is nothing about my identity that I know in a more primal way. . . . When someone . . . acts as though I'm not Nicholas's or Ruth's real mother. . . . I . . . resent that."[27]

Audrey T. Hingley continues this train of thought. "Don't tell adoptive parents to be hopeful for a child of their own; recognize that adoptive children are our own. Don't praise us for 'taking on someone else's child to raise,' because [they] are not 'someone else's'—they are ours."[28]

Dear Lord, have mercy on those who use words carelessly, including myself. Amen.
Prayer Focus: *For ability to speak the truth in love*

Affirmative Adoption Language, Continued

Adoptive parents can help their friends and family to "think it through" and change abusive to affirmative adoption language:

- "Yes, they have one daughter, *but* she was adopted." (As if that makes her not quite a daughter!) Better—"Yes, they have a daughter, whom they adopted." Better yet—"Yes, they have a daughter."

- "Do you know her *real* mother?" (As if the adoptive mother was not a real mother!) Better—"Do you know her birthmother (or first mother)?"

- "Adam is in trouble: he's adopted, you know." (As though adoption was the cause of the trouble!) Other children get in trouble, too—and at a higher rate, according to a juvenile court judge of Detroit, Michigan.[29]

- "She is an adopted child." Adoption is a process. It describes an action—not a person—and should not be used as a label. We don't say, "She is a cesarean child," when referring to another type of childbearing. Better—"She *was* adopted."

- "Do they have any children of their own?" (As if their children by adoption are not their own!) Better—"Do they also have children by birth?"

- "Are your children related?" (As if adoption doesn't really make families!) Better—"Are your children genetically related?" Better yet—call attention to some similarity, and say, "It's easy to see you come from the same family!"

- "How good of you to adopt!" (Why? How would you respond to someone who says, "How good of you to conceive!" or "How generous of you to bear more children!"?) Better—"You're a happy family." Or say something general about the blessings of having children.

- "Have you told them they were adopted?" (As if it's a secret!) Better—"Do you celebrate adoption days in your family like birthdays?"

- "Now that you've adopted, you'll probably conceive." (Yes, conception does sometimes occur after adoption, but research shows no basis for concluding adoption aids conception). Better—"Are you hoping for more children?"

- "How could any woman relinquish a child?" a letter from a mother in a syndicated column asked. She went on to say, "It takes a courageous and unselfish woman to give up a child she cannot care for, and it takes precious little character to get an abortion instead." Better—"I'm sure it took a lot of thought for the birthmother to choose adoption for her child."

- "Our child came by that trait honestly!" (What does that mean? Did my children come by certain traits dishonestly?) Better—omit the connotations and simply say, "It's obvious where that comes from!"

One Day at a Time

See how the lilies of the field grow. They do not labor or spin. Yet I tell you that not even Solomon in all his splendor was dressed like one of these. If that is how God clothes the grass of the field, which is here today and tomorrow is thrown into the fire, will he not much more clothe you, O you of little faith?
Matthew 6:28-30

March brought our family a medical crisis on top of other grief and loss. Finally I described my panic to the Lord in the form of a nightmare. Emerging from a cave with our children following us, Paul and I faced menacing threats. SICKNESS, UNBELIEF, SELFISHNESS, DRUG ABUSE, MATERIALISM, ADULTERY, TORTURE, REJECTION, VIOLENCE, WITCHCRAFT, FOUL LANGUAGE, and many other murky shadows claimed the territory through which we had to pass.

My husband stood firm and resolved to go forward, but I cowered. How could I lead our precious children down this path of life when evil surrounded us. Worst of all, a sense of my own weakness paralyzed me with fear of leading them astray myself. While looking dejectedly at the slime ahead of us, I noticed a clear footprint . . . and another. . . . They defined a trail. I recognized them at once, for there was blood in each print.

Then I turned to Matthew 6:25-34 and read Jesus' words which tell us not to worry about tomorrow. I concluded my quiet time with the prayer that God would help me with the tasks that needed doing for that day. I prayed he would help me follow in his footsteps, one at a time.

The problems didn't disappear right away, but bolstered with Scripture, prayer, telephone calls, letters, and love from friends and family, we were able to walk right through them. I believe it was a miracle from God that our son was able to undergo a series of complicated medical tests with a good attitude and total cooperation.

Jesus, thanks so much for marking a trail. Thanks for family and friends who walk beside us. Thanks for holding us when we can no longer walk. Amen.
Prayer Focus: *For those who are fearful of the problems of our age.*

Overheard in an Orchard

Said the Robin to the Sparrow, "I should really like to know why these anxious human beings rush around and worry so."

Said the Sparrow to the Robin, "Friend, I think that it must be that they have no Heavenly Father such as cares for you and me."[30]

—*Elizabeth Cheney*

MY SON GROWS UP

My hands were busy through the day,
I didn't have much time to play
The little games you asked me to.
But when you'd bring your teddy bear
And ask me please to share your fun,
I'd say; "A little later, son."
I'd tuck you in all safe at night
And hear your prayers, turn out the light.
Then tiptoe softly to the door. . . .
I wish I'd stayed a minute more.
For life is short, the years rush past. . . .
A little boy grows up so fast.
No longer is he at your side,
His precious secrets to confide.
The teddy bears are put away,
There are no longer games to play,
No good-night kiss, no prayers to hear. . . .
That all belongs to yesteryear.
My hands, once busy, now are still.
The days are long and hard to fill.
I wish I could go back and do
The little things you asked me to.[31]

I hope my children look back on today and see a mother who had time to play. Later there will be years for cleaning and cooking, for children grow up while we're not looking.

A New Line of Blessing

Our God, however, turned the curse into a blessing.
Nehemiah 13:2b.

The lights were off one night when six-year-old Jonathan called through the darkness. "Mommie, I can't sleep tonight." A childish wrong kept peace at bay, and he struggled for ten minutes to fully confess it.

Paul and I immediately assured him that every person confronted the same thing. Then we told him stories of our own failings in childhood.

"Did you really do that, Mommie?" Jonathan asked.

I told of guilt and sadness and how glad I was that Jesus could wash us where even soap and water could not. Amazed that we could identify with him in his need of forgiveness, Jonathan relaxed.

Then Paul prayed a simple prayer which Jonathan eagerly repeated. God's presence filled the room, and those moments remain a sweet memory to us.

As Christian parents, we can empathize with our children when they confront temptations. Lessons from our moral victories and defeats are part of their spiritual heritage and can strengthen them.

We can take this one step farther. Scripture suggests sin can affect families for generations. This means we should pray for release even from the sins of past generations whose effects on us we may not fully understand. Adoptive parents can pray for freedom for our children from weaknesses in our backgrounds as well as their biological heritage. We can help them establish a new line of God's blessing through obedience to God's Word.

Dear Lord, thank you for calling our children to follow you at an early age. Their sincere faith humbles me. Help Paul and me to strengthen them so that they can turn life's temptations into areas of spiritual strength. Amen.

Prayer Focus: *That our children might always be able to recognize sin, be quick to repent it, and use temptation to draw closer to God*

TWO PRAYERS

Last night my little boy confessed to me
Some childish wrong,
And kneeling at my knee,
He prayed with tears—
"Dear God, make me a man
Like Daddy—wise and strong:
I know you can."

Then while he slept
I knelt beside his bed,
Confessed my sins,
And prayed with low-bowed head,
"O God, make me a child
Like my child here—
Pure, guileless,
Trusting thee with faith sincere."[32]

—Andrew Gillies

LITTLE THINGS

Little drops of water, little grains of sand,
Make the mighty ocean and the pleasant land.
So the little moments, humble though they be,
Make the mighty ages of eternity.
So our little errors lead the soul away
From the path of virtue, far in sin to stray.
Little deeds of kindness, little words of love,
Help to make earth happy like the heaven above.[33]

—Julia A. Carney

A Strong Tradition

God did not give us a spirit of timidity, but a spirit of power,
of love and of self-discipline.
2 Timothy 1:7

"You never know what you'll get when you adopt," a woman once declared in my presence. I thought of asking if she knew what characteristics her children, whom she conceived, would bring with them.

Abraham Lincoln is quoted as saying, "Everything I am or ever hope to be, I owe to my angel mother." I assume he was speaking about his second mother.

Gerald Rudolph Ford, Sr., adopted a baby and married the baby's mother. He gave the child his name, nurtured him, and produced a president of the United States.

George Bush relates he gained some of his grandchildren through adoption. This helped change his thinking about abortion.

Among many Olympic champions who claim adoption, Greg Lougains, part Samoan by birth, overcame dyslexia, other handicaps, and racial barriers. Winning a silver medal at age sixteen in 1976, then two gold medals in both 1984 and 1988, he is considered one of the greatest divers in history.

Kitty and Peter Carruthers, brother and sister ice-skaters, stole hearts as well as world championships in 1984. They celebrate their adoptions and speak at Adoption Advocacy Training Institutes.

Paul and Clara Jobs adopted Steve in 1955. He co-invented the Apple computer.

Pearl Buck, George and Gracie Burns, Bob Hope, Ann Keimel Anderson, Bill Myers, and Dorothy and Bob DeBolt, Roy and Dale Evans Rogers are all adoptive parents.

Next time I hear, "You never know what you'll get when you adopt," I won't point out the fallacy of their reasoning. I might agree. "Right! You may get a president. . . . Or an Olympic gold medal winner. . . . Or the child you've always dreamed of!"

Dear God, thank you that adoptive families stand in a strong tradition and that adoption has blessed families throughout history and in every walk of life. Please help clear up confusion and worry surrounding it, so it can be seen as your provision for meeting needs. Amen.

Prayer Focus: *For truth about adoption to prevail*

Research Shows Adoption Works for All

An article in *National Adoption Reports* notes research indicating that adoption benefits key parties affected by adoption, including the child and both adoptive and biological parents. Studies of adolescents by Leslie M. Stein and Janet L. Hoopes challenge negative myths about adoptees and suggests they develop normal identities and understandings of who they are.

These researchers say that "contrary to expectations, significant differences were not found in the expected direction between the two groups. More specifically, adopted subjects showed no deficits in functioning on measures of overall identity when compared to their non-adoptive counterparts." Even more impressive is the fact that "higher scores on one of the identity measures were obtained by the adoptive group."[34]

Pharaoh's Daughter

A Reading based on Exodus 2—12

Only a mother with empty arms, who has hidden beneath the palm trees at fertility festivals and cries into her mat at night . . . who recognizes that her own longing, her own nature unfulfilled, is the ultimate enemy . . . whose empty arms ache until they ask to be cut off if they can never hold her baby—only she can know what the first sight of my son meant to me.

I was still young then, but already there were questions. And there were answers. The gods were displeased. Soon magicians would be called and remedies prescribed.

I wore the coveted title, "Daughter of the Sun God," and held the admiration of visiting royalty as well as the subjects in my father's kingdom. But I would have traded it all for the life of a Hebrew slave women in the kingdom's northern province, just to touch, to love, and to watch a son or daughter grow. Though poor and miserable—how rich those women were! Their god blessed them with fertility, which enraged and frightened my father.

One day, when the chariot of the sun rolled high overhead, I summoned my servants for bathtime. They selected rich spices, soft garments, and jeweled combs—a whole entourage of supplies.

The waters were warm, and the maids selected a favorite bathing site of mine among the bullrushes on the northern bank of the Nile River. I recall that last, casual walk down the footpath. I remember the next scenes, etched like the finest hieroglyphs in my memory: a sheepherder's quaint basket floating among the bulrushes. My shaking hands as my servant held it out to me. The strength of that baby's cry. His eyes. And the pounding of my heart.

The sun's chariot must have stopped, for I held my baby's kicking body against my heart for a long time. Yes, the chariot must have stopped, for the gods transformed me. They wakened meaning in my life. They put strength into my arms. I blessed the gods of the river, the gods of the sun, and the gods of the bulrushes which had brought this child to me.

And I named him "Moses—the One I Have Drawn from the River." I knew with more certainty than I knew my name that he was mine—brought to me by the gods.

The chariot of the sun stopped for us. When it began to roll again, I sensed his needs, his hunger. The basket . . . I looked at the basket and felt compassion for the woman who had carefully woven it, plastered it with pitch, and lined it with rags. I could see her careful plan, her strength, and her desperation to save her son.

Yes, rumors about a death-decree must have been true. Hatred toward the decree which had threatened this child's life welled up in me. (I should have known that because I broke his law, people would say I was not Pharaoh's daughter . . . that they would pronounce "Daughter of the Sun God" with scorn instead of reverence.)

My maids, spellbound until then, gasped as a young Hebrew girl jumped from the grasses, reeds, and bulrushes. "He's hungry," she blurted, without deference to dignitaries. Then embarrassed at implying my breasts couldn't satisfy him, she suggested the obvious—a wet nurse.

I looked at her. "What is your name?"

"Miriam," she answered simply. She didn't have to explain. I knew. She knew. She had witnessed the rescue—had helped her family plan it.

"Yes," I agreed. "Feed my son, and bring him to me again."

I returned to the palace, but its glory evaded me as I planned for the education of my son. In becoming a mother to a Hebrew (in defiance of my father's law), I loosened the grip of his hierarchy, his kingdom, and his gods upon my life.

During the short years of Moses' infancy and nursing, while he returned with his sister to his Hebrew family, he gained an amazing belief in one God who called an ancestor, Abraham, to follow him in faith. As Moses grew, he and I wondered what our "calling" was.

From his first insistent cries, I knew Moses would be a leader. But before he had a chance to prove himself, he took justice into his own hands and killed an Egyptian who had abused a Hebrew. How could I accuse him? I too had defied Egyptian law.

The years had built up to that day. Moses completely rejected his title, "Son of the Sun-God's Daughter." My own title, "Pharaoh's Daughter," had lost meaning for me long before. He ran, and I went into hiding.

Pharaohs came and went. My kingdom was gone. My son was gone. My gods were gone. I longed for something . . . felt drawn toward something. . . . And I waited.

During Moses' exile, I learned more about Hebrew beliefs. They contended it was faith in one God, more than bloodlines, which established citizenship in their community. Through the years a number of Egyptians had joined the Hebrew ranks, completely identifying with them (Exod. 12:48-49).

I wondered which was reality: so many gods—the snakes, the water, the sun—or one God, above and creator of everything else? Motherhood, my introduction to Hebrewness, strengthened my skepticism of Egyptian beliefs. It gave me courage to examine the strange, simplistic-sounding belief in one God.

I was an old woman when Moses returned with a shepherd's staff in his hand. His former self-assured confidence was gone. In its place was a power he said came from God. I watched as plague after plague pounded the new pharaoh's empire. That's when I knew for sure the gods had—No! that God had called us for a special purpose and the gods I had once served were only imitations.

On the night of God's wrath, when the sons of the Egyptians were killed, the blood of lambs saved all of us who placed it on our doorposts. The Hebrews and "strangers" who did experienced great deliverance under the leadership of Moses, whom I had drawn from the water.

The God of the water, of the bulrushes, of fertility, and all nature—the one who rides the Chariot of the Sun—smiled on us. He parted the Red Sea. Soon after, Moses wrote down hundreds of laws God spoke to him. His training was well used. My mother's heart was deeply satisfied. As I came to the end of my earthly life, I had not only a son. I had a people. I had a God.

—Vernell Klassen Miller

Family Life

"You shall raise up the foundations of many generations."
Isaiah 58:12 (NRSV)

The Lord will guide you
  continually,
 and satisfy your needs in
  parched places,
 and make your bones strong;
 and you shall be like a watered
  garden,
  like a spring of water,
  whose waters never fail.
 Your ancient ruins shall be rebuilt;
  you shall raise up the
  foundations of many
  generations;
 you shall be called the repairer of
  the breach,
  the restorer of streets to live in.

—Isaiah 58:11-12, NRSV

What Makes Adoptive Grandparents Special?

"Children's children are a crown to the aged,
and parents are the pride of their children."
Proverbs 17:6

What makes adoptive grandparents special? All the usual things, of course—like frying pancakes into rabbit shapes or playing harmonica to put a restless one to sleep. But hidden among these already-shiny moments are treasures which can only be captured by the sensitive ears of adoptive parents. For example—

When Grandma Klassen had her bags packed for over a year and stayed near the telephone because her daughter was expecting a baby, and she could get a call any day.

When Grandpa Miller heard we were expectant parents on a waiting list for adoption and said, "Oh, good! I hope it's a boy! I've always wanted a Miller grandson!"

When grandparents say their grandchildren obviously belong in the family because of similar characteristics, or when they identify with them so closely that they sometimes call them by a cousin's name. (I have seen this type of identification in interracial adoptive families also.)

When a child behaves a certain way, and they say, "You'd expect that—being your child!"

When a man asks his dad if he could accept a child of another race as a grandchild, and his dad replies, "If he's your child—well, then, that makes him our grandchild!"

I just hung up the phone from visiting with my mother and father. I told them I was working on a book for Herald Press. "What's the name of it?" Mom wanted to know.

"Meditations for Adoptive Parents," I enthusiastically replied.

Silence. Then she wondered, "But how would they be any different?"

I love her for that!

Thank you, God, for grandparents and for the unique manner in which they instill values, heritage, and faith through love. I'd like you to inscribe these moments on my children's hearts, like shining stars to guide them through all their life's journeys. Amen.

Prayer Focus: *Gratitude for grandparents*

PRAYER

I shall pass through this world only once. If, therefore, there be any kindness I can show or any good thing I can do, let me do it now. Let me not defer or neglect it. For I shall not pass this way again.[35]

—*Grellet*

THE BRIDGE BUILDER

An old man going a lone highway came at the evening, cold and grey, to a chasm vast and wide and steep, with waters rolling cold and deep. The old man crossed in the twilight dim: the sullen stream had no fears for him; but he turned when safe on the other side and built a bridge to span the tide.

"Old man," said a fellow pilgrim near, "you are wasting your strength with building here. Your journey will end with the ending day: you never again will pass this way. You've crossed the chasm, deep and wide. Why build you this bridge at eventide?"

The builder lifted his old grey head. "Good friend, in the path I have come," he said, "there followeth after me today, a youth whose feet must pass this way. The chasm that was as nought to me—to that fair-haired youth, may a pitfall be: he, too, must cross in the twilight dim. Good friend, I am building this bridge for him."[36]

—*Will Allen Dromgoole*

The Road

"Impress them [these commandments] on your children.
Talk about them when you sit at home and when you walk along the road,
when you lie down and when you get up."
Deuteronomy 6:7

I tend to act in response to two fears—that my children will be undisciplined or overdisciplined. Growing up without restrictions can spring traps snaring a person for life. Yet children need freedom and practice in making their own choices.

Our guidebook instructs us to teach our children as we walk, sit, lie down, and get up. Hebrews 12:5-11 holds a poignant message for adoptive parents in particular. "What son is not disciplined by his father? If you are not disciplined . . . (then you are illegitimate children)." We can adopt our children legally, assuming all rights of parenthood. We can receive the blessings of church and society in child consecration, at baby showers, in daily encounters. We can bond as strongly as other families. But establishing parenthood after God's example also requires assuming the responsibility of discipline.

I note with alarm the increasing tendency to view all punishment for wrongdoing as being abusive. Whether their children were conceived within their marriage or adopted, if parents do not establish godly direction and authority in their home, they do not achieve true parenthood.

Lord, I want to be a parent after your example. I desire true freedom for my children. Please help them to sense at an early age that such freedom can come only through obedience to you. Amen.

Prayer Focus: *That parents will lead their children in the paths of righteousness*

DO NOT CONFUSE

When parents confuse overindulgence for generosity, they teach their children to be selfish.

When parents use anger in place of authority, their parenting becomes unreasonable, and they wonder why their children fear them.

When parents equate all discipline with abuse, they relax standards and wonder why their children are uncontrollable.

When parents forget to give the gift of laughter, life becomes a burden to little hearts.

When parents fear the show of affection, they deprive their children of a sense of worth.

When parents believe that saying "no" will wound a child's spirit, they become slaves and allow their children to become tyrants.

When parents push their children go row up, they hurry a childhood, which can never be regained.

When parents refuse to relinquish responsibility, they thwart their children's growth.

When parents expect perfection from their children, they sow seeds of discouragement, depression, and defeat.

When parents forget to pray, their children may forget God.[37]

—Aviva Joy

Gethsemane

*All you who pass by. . . . Look and see if there
is any sorrow like my sorrow.*
Lamentations 1:12, NRSV

Kate cuddled her new son in her lap and gently stroked his fuzzy head. How terrible it was when she placed him into his new mother's arms. She could not have begun to imagine what pain and grief lay ahead—hours of heart-wrenching sobs and empty, aching arms that could still feel the weight of the tiny body. Kate's pain carved a deep well which now holds more of God's love—pure water from which others can drink.[38]

When I read Kate's story in a Christian magazine, it reminded me of my frequent pauses to pray beside my sleeping children. Gratitude fills my heart and overflows, leaving their plump cheeks wet with both my kisses and my tears. Sometimes sorrow mingles with gratitude—sorrow that I wasn't the one who had the privilege of conceiving and bearing them. This love draws me to Gethsemane where I lay my need to be everything to my children at the cross.

When I visited with Ann Keimel Anderson last summer, she said adoptive parents tend to deny grief. But it is at this point that honesty could open the way for our children to be honest—for they may need to visit Gethsemane some day, too. Certainly not all relinquishing and adoptive parents or their children feel this type of loss and sorrow. But those of us who do can kneel beside our Savior in the garden.

Jesus, I have always found you here, praying, "Nevertheless, not my will, but thine be done." Help me to make that my prayer, too. Amen.
Prayer Focus: *For my friends who are facing their own trials*

*All those who journey, soon or late,
Must pass within that garden gate—
Must kneel alone in darkness there
And battle with some fierce despair.*[39]

—Author unknown

True Love

"More tears have been shed over this piece of paper than over any other," a social worker told us as she reviewed the steps in adoption. She referred to a document titled, "Mother's voluntary relinquishment of care, custody and control, and parental rights, consent to adoption, waver of notice, and consent to order."

A similar paper to be signed by the birthfather concludes with, "He hereby voluntarily and irrevocably consents in writing that he has no parental rights to said dependent child."

Denial of our own preference for the good of another is a test of true love. The birthparents' relinquishment of parenting rights is matched by the adoptive parents' relinquishment of their rights to give children their genetic heritage. As the children mature, they learn that their rights to be brought up by the same people who gave them birth have been terminated.

There are some positive trends which allow relinquishment and adoption (and the attendant gains and losses) to be understood more completely than in the past. Information is more freely exchanged today than a generation ago. Medical history is now mandated in most states. Information about physical features, personality, hobbies, and vocational choices are more readily available. Today's adoptive parents tend more systematically to teach their children about adoption, beginning with the first questions about babies. This prevents the trauma which often accompanied "the telling" at an older age. It also lays a foundation of honesty and trust.

Within this framework, the terminating of rights can be submitted to the Lord. When adoption is seen as God working things out for good (Rom. 8:28), then deferring for the sake of another becomes an action of love—even joy. My Anabaptist heritage underlines Jesus' teaching on servanthood and submission to others in the body of Christ. It follows that Christians will focus more on being servants, less on asserting "rights."

Childhood—an Inner Vest

"My soul is restless until it finds its rest in thee."
St. Augustine

The R. A. and Selma Strausz-Klassen home will always be the womb from which I sprang. I can reject its values, embrace it, deny it, affirm it, veer away, or return to it. But theirs will always be my childhood home and a basic part of my identity. I wear those early years, as everyone else does, for better or worse, like an inner vest wherever I go.

The search for personal identity stems, I suppose, from Adam and Eve's alienation from God. Until we find peace with God, we sense a missing piece in our life and relentlessly strive to fill the void. In adoption, the missing pieces of heredity may taunt a person with the promise of fulfillment. Curiosity about biological roots is normal, but it is only one facet in the total quest for self-understanding.

I expect God will call our children to himself at every stage of their lives. They may journey in diverse routes to answer that call. On the other hand, they may not.

I simply wish to put the overemphasized adoption search into perspective. It is neither a magical fairy nor a hideous monster. The notion that finding someone or a missing family tree will bring ultimate fulfillment to a person who has been adopted is a myth. It is also a myth that any other person or family can replace the childhood of one's children.

Dear Lord, our children's biological origins are different from ours. Help us to look at that issue with our children, neither bamboozled by its secrets nor terrorized by its threats. To have my children find wholeness—that is my goal as a parent. Enable me to start them out on that journey with confidence. Help me release them more fully into your care at each stage of development. Amen.

Prayer Focus: *For those searching for identity*

Why Is the Search Overdramatized?

One percent of all eligible adoptees applied to Minnesota's registry in its first two years of operation. In Pennsylvania, during a one-year access period, about 2 percent applied. A ten-year study in Scotland, which has a long-standing tradition of open records for adults, found that each year only an average of 1.5 adult adoptees *per 1,000* requested information—and many of them, merely for information on heritage.[40]

Only a tiny percentage of people who were adopted search for their biological parents. Then why is the search overdramatized?

For those whose primary conceptualization of family relatedness is based on biology, adoption holds discomforting assumptions and compelling questions. How can it work? Won't certain voids be felt?

The adoption search especially seems to hold fascination for those who have not experienced adoption. It symbolizes their own search for clues to their identity—as if someone else's puzzle of adoption could be solved, then, somehow, their life's puzzle might be also.

When Adoption Doesn't Work

Blessed are those who mourn, for they will be comforted.
Matthew 5:4

"Our giving these children a home didn't seem to make a difference in their lives," a woman sadly told me about the four children she and her husband had adopted.

I did not tell her about the statistics which show adoption to be predominantly positive. I did not remind her that many biologically-built families also fall apart nor that miracles have occurred in other families who have adopted formerly abused children. For her, "Adoption doesn't work."

There are birthmothers who felt pressure to relinquish and later regretted. For them, "Adoption doesn't work." Some people who have been adopted bear scars from inadequate bonding or perceived deficiencies. When breaks in human relationships hit your family, it feels like total failure.

I grieve that the most wonderful of God's creations, the family (no matter how it is built), doesn't always work. Human beings are made from clay and easily broken. My tears are near the surface when I hear of heartbreak in adoption, because I know that everyone involved acutely wanted it to work—wanted it to be a blessing.

Statistics or even a different perspective don't help much. What I can share, however, is that I too have experienced failures. And God has been with me then as well as in times of success. He is my comforter as well as my giver of joy.

I can also share the experience of a dear friend, an adoptive mother whose daughter had experienced sexual abuse in her first home. Her daughter found it nearly impossible to reciprocate love.

"I understand God's commitment to us better, now," my friend told me. "I'll just keep on loving, even if I can't expect any expression of love in return."

That's the kind of attitude to which we can all aspire.

Holy Comforter, for those who have been hurt in adoptive situations—touch their grief and transform it into a deeper understanding of your love. Amen.

Prayer Focus: *For those whose adoptions "didn't work"*

Only one life, 'twill soon be past;
Only what's done for Christ will last.[41]

—from a plaque

True evangelical faith
Cannot lie dormant.
It clothes the naked,
It feeds the hungry,
It comforts the sorrowful,
It shelters the destitute,
It serves those who harm it,
It binds up wounds,
It has become all things
To all men.[42]

—*Menno Simons, 1539*

"God has not called me to be successful.
He has called me to be faithful."[43]

—*Mother Teresa of Calcutta*

Abundant Life

The Lord God formed the man from the dust of the ground and breathed into
his nostrils the breath of life, and the man became a living being.
Genesis 2:7

Susan Viguers, in her book *With Child,* introduces us to daughter Ruth, who failed to thrive as an infant in an orphanage. At five and a half months, she looked like a newborn. She didn't cry. She scarcely even moved until her adoptive parents came.

Ruth drank only a little of formula and food dribbled out of her mouth. Susan, longing for her daughter's life, tried to feed her. The care Susan and Ken continued to give Ruth was similar to what she had previously received, but there was a difference now. Someone needed Ruth. Somehow she knew she had "come home" to her parents.

Ruth began to eat and move and steadily gained strength. Susan describes the powerful bonding process that emerged as she enabled life to fill Ruth's body and she became Ruth's mother. (This phenomenon happens repeatedly. A friend of mine describes her children, who were adopted as a sibling group, as blossoming in their new home.)[44]

Love is life-giving. To bond is to give love and life freely. Parents can sense the transmission of human life. Many parents assume it depends on a biological process. Adoptive parents know it is largely dependent on love. Susan calls it a "primal knowing" that we are our children's parents. Their bodies didn't come from us. But in an important sense their life does.

When God breathed the breath of life into Adam, I believe it was the breath of love. Without it our souls—sometimes even our bodies—die.

Heavenly Father, you made my body in secret and gave me a soul and a spirit.
Then you blessed me with a family which breathed love into my growing from and enabled me to live. I will pass these special love-traits to my children. Help me impart abundant life to them. Amen.
Prayer Focus: *For the channels of life-giving love to flow freely in our families*

Hugs and Kisses

Disbelief, excitement, panic, and an assorted variety of other strange and wonderful emotions rocked my sanity when our first child arrived. I functioned in a daze, so I wasn't sure I comprehended everything at the community baby shower. Sally exclaimed how smart Jonathan would be and what tremendous potential he had.

"How can you tell?" (I was sure she was right, but I wondered how anyone but his mother could be so sure.)

"Well, I know his parents," she said matter-of-factly.

Then I knew for sure I wasn't connecting properly, because everyone in town was aware that we were adopting—not giving birth. "But the limit of potential intelligence is largely inherited." I tried to sound coherent.

"No, it isn't!" she insisted. "Don't you know? It comes from hugs and kisses!"

I have been a mother now for over eight years. From my own experience, from others' testimonies, and from articles I have read, I conclude Sally is absolutely right!

Successful Parenting

For I am convinced that neither death nor life, neither angels nor demons,
neither the present nor the future, nor any powers, neither height nor depth,
nor anything else in all creation, will be able to separate us from
the love of God that is in Christ Jesus our Lord.
Romans 8:38-39.

"There's something we need to talk about," a friend said. She reported an ugly threat which our darling, three-year-old daughter made. "I thought you ought to know this, because you're Christians and what your children do affects your witness."

Many adoptive mothers and fathers believe God chose them as their children's parents. Yet within that "givenness," there remains the burden of doing a good job, of filling our sons' and daughters' childhoods with every form of godliness.

All parents can tell of regrets and fears as well as pride and hopes. Alas! I stand with those who either excessively worry or carry inordinate pride. When our children err, I feel like a failure as a parent, a person, and a Christian. I worry they may have ruined their lives forever. When they overcome, find success, or simply do a good job, I soar.

I find a measure of balance in Scripture. While never minimizing the importance of the parental role, the Bible offers it as only one ingredient in any persons's life. God's love goes before us, follows us, undergirds us, and hovers over us. Psalm 139 proclaims that there is nowhere we can go—not even hell—to hide from God. There are no lengths to which God is not willing to go to redeem our mistakes. This recurring theme enables me to walk more confidently in parenting.

Another ingredient in family life is free will. Adam and Eve, God's first human children were placed in a perfect environment with no phobias, hang-ups, codependencies, or health problems. Yet they chose to rebel. How arrogant, then, my exaggerated sense of responsibility must seem to the Lord—in whose hands lie our children's futures.

Dear Lord, forgive. Forgive the arrogance, the pride, the worry. Forgive my fears and demands of perfection both of myself and of our children. Help me balance the responsibility of parenthood with your all-powerful, ever-present love. And while I recognize the gift of choice, I pray—Oh, how I pray!—that our children will choose to follow you. Amen.
Prayer Focus: *For scriptural balance in parenting*

THE LOVE OF GOD

The love of God is greater far
Than tongue or pen can ever tell;
It goes beyond the highest star
And reaches to the lowest hell.
The guilty pair, bowed down with care,
God gave His Son to win;
His erring child He reconciled
And pardoned from his sin.

When hoary time shall pass away,
And earthly thrones and kingdoms fall;
When men who here refuse to pray,
On rocks and hills and mountains call;
God's love, so sure, shall still endure,
All measureless and strong;
Redeeming grace to Adam's race—
The saints' and angels' song.

Could we with ink the ocean fill,
And were the skies of parchment made;
Were every stalk on earth a quill,
And every man a scribe by trade;
To write the love of God above,
Would drain the ocean dry;
Nor could the scroll contain the whole,
Though stretched from sky to sky.

O love of God, how rich and pure!
How measureless and strong!
It shall forevermore endure—
The saints' and angels' song.[45]

—F. M. Lehman, 1917

Adoptive Parenting

He will cover you with his feathers, and under his wings you will find refuge;
his faithfulness will be your shield and rampart.
Psalm 91:4

I hoped the judge would not read the legal decree aloud at the finalization of Jonathan's adoption. It coldly declared that this child was deprived, parental rights had been terminated, and he was a ward of the court.

That offended me. My heart insisted my son had been my son from the moment of conception. No, even before then—from the time of my first prayers for children. There had never been a moment in his existence that I had not been waiting for him, hoping for him, calling him home.

Mercifully, the judge in our case omitted much technical language. Both of our children's adoption days in court were pure celebrations.

Several years later, I researched to broaden my perspectives for these meditations. I looked at adoption from many vantage points. They have one thing in common: a bough broke. A cradle fell. While researching, I mourned. And was comforted.

I will grieve with my children if they feel sad on realizing that a severing took place before the grafting which we celebrate. Or if some phrase on a legal document, an idle word, or a question with obscure answers brings them pain.

Then I will comfort them with God's Word, which declares that God himself becomes father to the motherless and fatherless (Ps. 27:10 and 68:5). That he engraves them upon the palms of his hands and never forgets them (Isa. 49:15-16a). And that the guarding angels of children have direct access to the throne of God (Matt. 18:10).

And so God's roadmap proves reliable for all people traveling as families. Through it, we find the one who carries our provisions for the journey. And we can ask for wisdom, comfort, or grace in proportion to our need.

Father, you have supplemented my protection of my children with awareness of your own special blessings for them. You, who call birds south in winter and hold the earth in the palm of your hand, have also provided for the branch that breaks. Wrap your wings around our family and help us learn to fly like eagles. Amen.

Prayer Focus: *For sensitivity to unique needs in adoption and to God's provision*

THE GRAFTED BRANCH

The angels hold their breath
As the Master Gardener opens his shears
To sever a tender shoot
From a prize rose bush.

He moves precisely,
Leaving an open cut which will heal in time,
But always boast a scar
To tell of the sacrifice, the gift.

Then the Gardener carefully, carefully
Carries the young shoot and inserts it into an open cut
Made by deep longing and praying
In another parent plant.

The original rose bush, pruned,
Directs its energy more determinedly
And pleases the Master
With new beauty.

The chosen parent bush
Receives the little shoot
And responds
With new incentives for growth.

And the grafted shoot
Becomes a strong, flourishing branch,
Opening with hybrid vigor toward the heavens
A gorgeous rose.

The angels breathe again
And join in songs of praise to the Gardener,
Who plants, transplants, prunes, and grafts,
And always delights in His own.

—Vernell Klassen Miller

Homelife

"Whatever you do, work at it with all your heart,
as working for the Lord, not for men."
Colossians 3:23

I come from a family of hard workers. I worked too, but my early addiction to words and reading got in the way. I kept books tucked under the bed, inside the cupboard, and behind the sofa. No matter what my assigned task, I was always ready to keep up with two or three other worlds. Some of those dear to me wish I had more of Martha's concern for dishes, cleaning, and laundry. I continue to struggle with this weakness. Now it is highlighted by my efforts to teach our children to do their share of work.

Sister Mary John Scherer, a Catholic nun whose face glows with purpose, taught an education class when I was earning my elementary teaching certificate. She led in prayer before beginning the morning lessons. Often she told the Lord, "We offer the work we do in this class as a prayer to you."

Work as a prayer? I had never thought of it like that before. Usually the goal I sought motivated me to take the steps necessary to attain it. I assumed my love for my children would automatically inspire me to keep up with added responsibility and to provide a shining house, luscious meals, and well-mended clothes.

Reality hit. Becoming a mother showed me I hadn't adequately dealt with procrastination, laziness, and selfishness. As intense as it is, love for my family does not totally equip me to complete my day-in, day-out responsibilities. I'd rather read!

I have to keep coming back to my commitment to follow Christ. As I remember Sister Mary John's prayer, I wonder if the work I do "says" anything to the Lord. If it is a form of prayer, what am I praying? Am I doing it for myself? For my family? Or "with all my heart," as unto him?

Father, I want to keep my first affection for you. Then I will be able to do a good job at whatever I do. Help me to learn life's lessons along with the children. (And, by the way, I'm thrilled they're learning to read!) Amen.

Prayer Focus: *That our work will please the Lord*

About Living

A moth lives just three or four days. Roaches live about twenty-six days, while the common snail lives two to three years. Lions live an average of thirty-five years, and bears average fifty years. A parrot will live to be around 100 years old. Elephants double that to 200 years. But we humans live forever, because we have an eternal soul.

A person's life on earth averages around seventy years. The Bible refers to the length of a full life for man as being three score and ten. The question is, just what do we do with those years? Several years ago, *Ladies Home Journal* published the following statistics showing the time used for activities by a person living seventy years.

Education would use up three years of the total. We spend an average of eight years on amusements. We eat for eight years. We spend eleven years at our work. We sleep for a total of twenty-four years. Washing and dressing use up about three and a half years. We walk for six years. We talk for three years. Reading takes three years of our life. We spend only half a year worshiping God, our Creator. . . .

"Do not work for food that spoils, but for food that endures to eternal life, which the Son of Man will give you. . . ." John 6:27[46]

—Ray Clark

Talent

Experts have concluded that if the net worth of all the elements of the human body were added up, the total would amount only to a few dollars. Yet our bodies are worthy to be the temple of the Holy Spirit. For the incalculable worth of a person's soul, Jesus Christ traded his heavenly throne for a cross.

Faith, Hope, and Love

And now these three remain: faith, hope and love.
But the greatest of these is love.
1 Corinthians 13:13

Even when our children are grown, and despite our mistakes, faith, hope, and love will continue. This poem by my father illustrates love stretching to include eternity.

LOVE

Love is like a rubber band
  That binds our hearts together;
Though it be stretched from land to land . . .
Its potent force cannot be broken.
  Its voice is clear though oft' unspoken.

This band that stretched to earth from heaven
  Still works great things as bread with leaven.

When that great trump of God shall sound,
  This cord that comes from God of love
Will fetch us from the barren ground
  And snap us back to our home above.
The bowstring drawn so tight through life
  Then sets us free from pain and strife.
As swift as an arrow we shall fly
  To meet our Savior in the sky.

May this cohesion never wane
  Till it effects a Wiedersh'n [a reuniting].[47]

—R. A. Klassen

Thank you, Lord, that Christians can anticipate unbroken fellowship forever.
Prayer Focus: *Gratitude for chords of love which cannot be broken*

If, for Adoptive Parents

If you can freely give children your heritage and graft them firmly into your family tree, and if you can point them to their first roots with honesty and gratitude—then you can parent with confidence, knowing you are offering a lifelong gift.

If you hope your children will mature into the likeness of Christ (even more than you desire them to resemble yourself)—then you have chosen the highest goal of parenthood.

If you listen to others describe the births of their children and feel just as proud of the way your children came, then you know the true meaning of "childbearing."

If you look stereotypes, false reports, and myths in the face and wonder what on earth they are talking about; if you can listen to thoughtless words of friends with patience, and say to yourself, *I will overlook that: they don't know how it sounds* (yet be able to discern the time to speak); and if you can read research and pseudo-research and sense any bias—then adoption had done more than bring you children. It has sharpened your ability to identify with minorities.

If you can step into a type of parenthood upon which society places a "role handicap," and not assimilate that perception into your own; if you have ever looked into the eyes of your child and known that he or she was always yours; if you have at the same time given thanks for another woman with whom you share the title of "mother"—then you can help your child build strong self-esteem.

If your heart swells with pride at your child's successes; if you hold that child when he or she fails; if you do not blame the failure on genetic origin nor blame yourself but "own" it because your child is yours; if you pray desperately for the salvation of your children, saying (like Moses did) that if they cannot join you in God's kingdom, you cannot go either—then you have learned to pray. Then parenthood has seeped into your soul, even if it didn't emanate from your body, and you will never *not* be a parent again.

If you rise each morning resolving to be an ideal parent but break your best intentions before noon, forced to acknowledge your humanness and humbly press on; if you offer your spouse and children the same forgiveness you receive from God; if you can point your children past your own sins toward God and his family—then you have truly become a parent. Then your family will be a beacon in a dark and lonely world.

May God go with you, and may you experience JOY!

—Vernell Klassen Miller

Our Father

A reading based on Matthew 1—2, 6:7-15, and Luke 2—3

She accepted my proposal! Mary would become my wife! The joy of anticipating marriage and family life made my work seem like play.

Then misunderstandings and confusion threw a wedge into my plans. An unexpected pregnancy and possible stoning hung over my beloved.

I tossed on my mat at night, heartbroken. Mary had seemed so sincere and pure. I reviewed my choices. I would not marry one who had obviously been unfaithful to me. On the other hand, I loved Mary. I didn't want harm to come to her.

Surely this was a nightmare. Our love couldn't be over. How could Jehovah allow this to happen to me? Or does he even hear and care? Four hundred years had passed since a prophet had claimed to have a word from God. Maybe he didn't speak to us anymore.

No, this decision would not be based on faith. It would be based on reasoning—cold, calculated reasoning. I was a righteous man. I intended to continue keeping the law, but my faith in Jehovah-Jirah, One Who Meets Our Needs, was shaken. Yes, that was the way it had to be. I would put Mary away privately and get it over with. Get back to the carpentry business. Forget marriage and sons and daughters. Maybe even God.

In the darkness of night—in a dream—an angel stood beside my mat. I saw him and wondered why he would come to one like me with so little faith. I scarcely had a name. People called me, "the carpenter."

But the angel spoke my name, "Joseph, son of David," like I was a prince, an actual son of King David! (He didn't mention my doubts and fears. It seemed he looked right past them and touched a favorite promise of Mary's and mine—that the Savior would come and save his people from their sins.)

"Don't hesitate to take Mary as your wife," the angel went on. "For the child within her has been conceived by the Holy Spirit. And she will have a son, and you shall name him Jesus, Immanuel—God With Us."

I woke and touched my mat, my beard, and the walls around me to check for reality. I stood. Everything had changed. Even the world—all history!—was different. The Messiah was arriving—and Mary and I were to be part of the drama!

It was more than my feeble mind could comprehend. Catapulted from despair into ecstasy, I wept. I laughed out loud, I danced, and wept again. Mary! My love, more precious to me now than ever before! What secret she had kept. What sorrow she must have borne at my not knowing. I shuddered at what horror could have met her. What was she doing now? Was she tired? Sick? Servant girls had no one to minister to them.

"Mary," I whispered the name to myself. "You and I will see the promise. Our son will be the son of the Most High."

Our son. Jehovah God had chosen to share his fatherhood with me—had sent an angel to tell me to give the Messiah a proper Jewish name and home. He would be born the son of a carpenter.

I wrapped an outer robe around myself and crept through the early dawn toward Mary's apartment. "Mary," I called softly.

Immediately she was at the door. We laughed, we cried, we praised the Lord.

"Come on, let's go home," I said at last. "After all, you are my engaged wife!"

I would have never planned things this way. I would have finished my apartment first and held a traditional wedding. We would have had a party—not with lavish, expensive food, but a celebration to consummate our courtship and physical love.

Instead, fatherhood was thrust on me—adoptive fatherhood to protect and nourish Israel's only hope for salvation. My fatherhood took Mary to a stable for the delivery, to Egypt to escape Herod's sword, then back to Nazareth for Jesus' childhood.

It was a delight to teach Jesus. He learned eagerly and studied the characteristics of wood. Our customers were pleased with our work. They said the yokes we made for their oxen were light and fit well. Someday Jesus would use the language of our trade to describe his own offer to share yokes and make burdens light. "Take my yoke upon you," he would say.

Mary and I often recounted the events of his conception and birth to Jesus. I sensed the importance of my role in modeling the love and protection of Jesus' heavenly Father. From what Mary and I could discern about our unusual son, he was born in every way a human—unaware, at first, of his divine, eternal existence. It was my privilege to lead him into maturity and help him discover his calling.

As Jesus reached manhood, he sensed his divine mission more clearly. He had always been an avid learner of the Torah, the Psalms of his ancestor David, and especially the Prophets. Then he studied each aspect of the deliverance from Egypt and the Passover tradition. After his twelfth birthday, we prepared him carefully for his own first Passover—an important milestone in every Jewish boy's life.

In retrospect, I shouldn't have been surprised that he stayed behind in the temple after the Passover, probing the teachers of the law with questions. Did he ask about the lambs which were sacrificed? Did he ask about prophecies pointing to the Lamb? What a holy and terrible day that must have been for him! He said something to me which indicated I had taught him well. He called the temple, "my Father's house." But Mary and I were too worried to feel pleased.

How we worried in those days that we would do a good job parenting, that we would point our son in the right direction, that we would be the type of parents he needed.

I didn't live long enough to walk beside Jesus during his final hours. He used the name he called me—"Abba" ("Daddy," always my favorite name)—when he called to God in the garden of Gethsemane. Nor did I fully comprehend that my adoption of Jesus was a pattern showing the whole world that our God is a Father who desires to adopt all those who believe in him, Jews and Gentiles alike, into his family.

What joy it would have given me to hear Jesus teach his friends that God was like a father! "Our Father in heaven," he once instructed them to pray—a new term for my people and a new way of praying.

What I lived in human weakness, loving Jesus and giving him my royal lineage, my name, my trade, likes and dislikes, and inheritance—God is doing in perfection for his people. He is making them not just servants or friends, but adopted children, royal sons and daughters, with full privileges as coheirs with Jesus.

Jesus was not begotten of my genes. I was not called to give him his human potential—only to develop and model for all generations "our Father which is in heaven."

—Vernell Klassen Miller

Acknowledgments

The publisher attempted to trace the ownership of all poems and quotations and to secure all necessary permissions from authors or holders of copyrights. Should there be any oversight in making proper acknowledgment, upon notification the publisher will correct such omissions in any future editions of this publication.

For permission to reprint from copyrighted works, the author and publisher are indebted to the sources listed below.

1. Shirley Collins, "Promises." Used by permission of the author.

2. Muriel B. Dennis, *Chosen Children*, compiled by Muriel B. Dennis (Good News Publishers: Westchester, Ill., 1978), footnote, p. 19.

3. Lois Raynor, *The Adopted Child Comes of Age* (London: George Allend and Unwin, Ltd., 1980), p. 111.

4. Colette Taube Dywasuk, *Adoption—Is It for You?* (New York: Harper and Row, 1973), p. 69.

5. Author unknown, "Passover for the Family," *Jewish Voice Broadcasts*, April, 1987, p. 5. Reprinted with permission of Jewish Voice Broadcasts, Inc.; P.O. Box 6; Phoenix, AZ 85001.

6. Margaret Munk, "On the Night of Andrew's Birth." Used by permission.

7. Karolyn Kelly-O'Keefe, "Learning to Soar," *Stepping Stones*, August-September 1991, p. 2.

8. Author unknown, "Legacy of an Adopted Child," quoted in Kathleen Silber and Phylis Speedlin, *Dear Birthmother* (San Antonio, Tex.: Corona Publishing Company, 1983), pp. 144-145. Used by permission of publisher.

9. Carol A. Hallenbeck, *Our Child: Preparation for Parenting in Adoption* (Wayne, Pa.: Our Child Press, 1984), pp. 11, 24.

10. Kathleen Silber and Phylis Speedlin, *Dear Birthmother* (San Antonio, Tex.: Corona Publishing Company, 1983), pp. 111-143, paraphrased and summarized.

11. Carol A. Hallenbeck, *Our Child: Preparation for Parenthood in Adoption—Instructor's Guide*, p. 53.

12. Dorothy W. Smith and Laurie Nehls Sherwen, *Mothers and Their Adopted Children: The Bonding Process* (116 Pinehurst Ave., New York City, N.Y. 10033: The Tiresias Press, Inc., 1988), p. 89.

13. Vernell Klassen Miller, "By What Authority?"

14. Open adoption and its effect on children as well as parents have been studied by Kraft, et al., in "Child and Adolescent Social Work Journal," 1985, cited in *Mothers and Their Adopted Children: The Bonding Process*, p. 175.

15. Fleur Conkling Heyliger, reprinted from *The Saturday Evening Post*, © 1952. Used by permission.

16. From a letter written by Donna Jean Breckenridge to *Stepping Stones*, August-September 1991, pp. 2-3.

17. Susan T. Viguers, *With Child* (Orlando: Harcourt, Brace, Jovanovich, 1986), p. 207.

18. Marilyn Black Phemister, "Tears in Season," *The Voice of the Windmill* (Wilson, N.C.: Star Books, 1988), p. 92. Used by permission.

19. "Are Adoptive Families Different? Researchers Say, 'Yes! They Are Better Adjusted,' " *National Adoption Reports*, May-June 1985, p. 3. Marquis and Detweiler's findings were published in the American Psychological Association's *Journal of Personality and Social Psychology,* and this article is based on that research report. Requests for reprints of the full article should be sent to Richard A. Detweiler, Department of Psychology, Drew University, Madison, NJ 07940.

20. Zola Levitt, *The Seven Feasts of Israel* (Dallas, Tex.: self-publication by Zola Levitt, 1979), pp. 1-31.

21. Mrs. Roman Liechty, "Hey, Mom! We're Home!" [Full author name and source unknown.]

22. Valorie Mills, McCracken, Kan., personal comment. Used by permission.

23. Eleanor Niemela Beachy, Pawnee Rock, Kan., personal comment. Used by permission.

24. These quotations come from written and oral interviews. Most were reported in Dorothy W. Smith and Laurie Nehls Sherwen, *Mothers and Their Adopted Children*.

25. Ibid.

26. Margaret Munk, "Kinship." Used by permission.

27. Susan T. Viguer, *With Child* (Orlando: Harcourt, Brace, Jovanovich, 1986), pp. 222-223.

28. Audrey T. Hingley, "What Makes Someone a Real Mother?" *Stepping Stones*, October-November 1988, pp. 1-2.

29. Colette Taube Dywasuk, *Adoption—Is It For You?* p. 149.

30. Elizabeth Cheney, "Overheard in an Orchard," from a plaque.

31. Author and title unknown. From a plaque.

32. Andrew Gillies, "Two Prayers," copied from an old scrapbook of poems, original source unknown.

33. Julia A. Carney, "Little Things" in Ord L. Morrow and John I. Paton, eds., *Poems for Sunshine and Shadow* (Lincoln, Neb.: Back to the Bible Publishers, 1962), p. 20. Reprinted by permission of the Good News Broadcasting Assoc., Inc. All Rights Reserved.

34. "Federal Statistician Finds Adoption Working for All," *National Adoption Reports*, July-August 1985, pp. 3-6.

35. Grellet, "Prayer," source unknown.

36. Will Allen Dromgoole, "The Bridge Builder," source unknown.

37. Aviva Joy, "Do Not Confuse." Used by permission of author.

38. From Charlotte H. Burkholder, *Christian Living*, September 1991, pp. 25-26.

39. Gethsemane, author unknown. Taken from the last verse of an old, anonymous poem.

40. Jacqueline Hornor Plumez, *Successful Adoption* (New York: Harmony Books, division of Crown Publishers, 1987), p. 122.

41. Author and title unknown. From a plaque.

42. Adapted from *The Complete Writings of Menno Simons*, translated by Leonard Verduin and edited by J. C. Wenger (Scottdale, Pa.: Herald Press, 1984) p. 307.

43. Mother Teresa is said to have made this comment to a reporter some years ago.

44. Susan T. Viguers, *With Child*, pp. 165-210.

45. F. M. Lehman, "The Love of God," *The Mennonite Hymnal* (Scottdale, Pa.: Herald Press, 1967), p. 538. Used by permission.

46. Ray Clark, "About Living," from notes of oral presentation on behalf of Standard Publishing Company heard by Vernell Klassen Miller.

47. R. A. Klassen, "Love," quoted in James R. Klassen, *Jimshoes in Vietnam* (Scottdale, Pa: Herald Press, 1986), p. 328. Used by permission.

The Author

Vernell Klassen Miller, her husband, Paul (both native Kansans), and children Jonathan (1984) and Elise (1987) farm near Hanston, Kansas. Vernell is a full-time homemaker and mother by choice. She also enjoys teaching Spanish to several home educating families, writing mini-dramas for special occasions in the Hanston Mennonite Church (to which the Millers belong), and involvement in church and community activities. Her free-lance writing includes poetry, meditations, human interest and family life features, and home-schooling topics.

Before their children came, Vernell taught in the public schools for four years. Prior to that, she and Paul worked in Mexico with Mennonite Central Committee. Some of the adventures of those years are chronicled in Vernell's first book, *Anywhere with You* (Herald Press, 1989).

Vernell attended Goshen (Ind.) College, earned a B.S. in home economics from Bethel College (North Newton, Kan.), and an elementary school teacher's certificate from Saint Mary of the Plains College (Dodge City, Kan.).